CHESTER HIMES

M.L. Wilson

MELROSE SQUARE PUBLISHING COMPANY
LOS ANGELES, CALIFORNIA

Senior Consulting Editor for Chelsea House
Nathan Irvin Huggins
Director
W.E.B. Du Bois Institute for Afro-American Research
Harvard University

Consulting Editors for Melrose Square
Raymond Friday Locke
Antony Stately

Cover Painting: Jesse J. Santos
Cover Design: Jeff Renfro

CHESTER HIMES

MELROSE SQUARE BLACK AMERICAN SERIES

CONTENTS

The Protest Writer's Dilemma

Chapter One

The Protest Writer's Dilemma

LATE IN THE spring of 1948, Chester Himes was invited to become a writer-in-residence at Yaddo, a prestigious artists' retreat in Saratoga Springs, New York. Consisting of a mansion and several studios on a lush, private estate, Yaddo housed and fed writers, painters, and composers for several months at a time, allowing them to pursue their art without interruption or financial constraint. An invitation to Yaddo was a kind of artistic seal of approval—particularly meaningful to a writer such as Himes because few blacks were asked to this predominantly white community.

Himes's reputation as a writer began to grow in 1944, shortly after he published his first novel at the age of 35. In recognition of his literary talent, he was invited to reside at Yaddo, a renowned artists' colony (shown here), four years later.

The 38-year-old Himes could hardly have anticipated that he would be invited to Yaddo as a published author given serious critical attention: His itinerant, pain-filled childhood and abortive academic career had led to a short-lived crime spree and a long term in prison that began when he was 19. He started to write short stories while he was serving his sentence.

Himes continued with his writing after he was released from prison more than seven years later, in 1936. While holding a series of manual labor jobs, he began to work on his first novel, *If He Hollers Let Him Go*. The book was published when he was 35 years old and quickly gained a reputation as one of the most powerful black protest novels to be published in the United States during the 1940s. Himes, who attributed most of the hardships in his life to the effects of racial prejudice, depicted the hopelessness of race relations in this frightening account of racism in America during World War II.

Because *If He Hollers Let Him Go* was a critical success, Himes was offered a contract to write a second novel, which he entitled *Lonely Crusade*. Published in 1947, it described the betrayal of a black union organizer by virtually everyone he knows—including members of his union, the Communist party,

Himes's belief that whites did not take the problems of blacks as seriously as they should spurred him to become one of the most vocal black protest writers in America.

his wife, his mistress, and (as often as not) himself. Whereas *If He Hollers Let Him Go* was highly praised, *Lonely Crusade* was widely criticized. Himes's second novel united blacks, whites, Communists, liberals, conservatives, and literary critics in condemning its author for his sharp opinions on racial relations.

Himes was subsequently forced to return to menial labor in order to support himself and his wife. He tried to work on a new novel, but it proved to be exceptionally difficult for him to find the time and energy to write while holding on to a job. Consequently, the invitation to stay at Yaddo was doubly rewarding to him. Yet he was unable to write there. He had been finding it difficult to write ever since *Lonely Crusade* had been given a horrendous reception.

During Himes's stay at Yaddo, the University of Chicago asked him to deliver a speech entitled "The Dilemma of the Negro Writer." Despite his troubles with his new novel, he had no difficulty in writing the speech. However, delivering it proved to be something of a problem. Before facing a predominantly white audience with what he knew would be an unpopular message, he nervously took two tablets of the amphetamine Benzedrine and drank some wine. He then proceeded to tell the truth as he saw it, as he had been telling it since he had first set pen to paper.

According to Himes, all black American writers in the 1940s faced conflicts within themselves because it was painful for them to tell the truth about racial oppression in the

United States. If they tried to mute their protests either by attempting to explain the suffering of blacks through the universal suffering of the human race or by looking back at their African heritage for an understanding of their present condition, they would betray their subject. The real reason for the oppression of blacks in America was the legacy of slavery and segregationist policies. Only an intensive look at these matters could provide insight into the lives of black Americans.

Not surprisingly, publishers were no more anxious to publish black protest novels than writers were to write them, Himes said. Uncompromising, bleak books were rarely profitable. Besides, editors were wary of black protest writers; most of the blacks whom editors knew personally were successful, well-educated, middle-class professionals whose lives appeared to be prejudice-free.

Himes told the audience that if a book by an honest black protest writer were to be published, the reactions of its readers were bound to be violent. Readers from the black middle class did not want to have their sufferings at the hands of whites portrayed because such portrayals might interfere with their being accepted by whites. Conversely, white readers did not want to face the feelings of guilt that such a book would foster.

Therefore, a writer such as Himes faced a dilemma; America demanded his truths yet rejected them. He said in his speech: "If this plumbing for the truth reveals within the Negro personality homicidal mania...a pathetic sense of inferiority...arrogance, Uncle Tomism, hate and fear and self-hate, this then is the effect of oppression on the human personality. These are the daily horrors, the daily realities, the daily experiences of an oppressed minority."

The audience greeted Himes's harsh recital with total silence. He reacted to this reception by spending the rest of the week in Chicago shying away from the controversy that his remarks had stirred up.

Back at Yaddo, Himes was still unable to write. That he would eventually become an extremely prolific writer seemed unimaginable at the time. His life was a long and lonely struggle for understanding and respect; attempting to attain acceptance and recognition—especially through writing—often proved to be difficult and wearying. Accordingly, his literary crusade against racism was marked at times by periods when he would ignore his writing completely.

Nevertheless, Himes managed to summon up the strength and desire to air his views in the years that followed his departure from Yaddo. Ultimately, he produced a number of popular works—including a series of novels that featured a pair of black detectives, Grave Digger Jones and Coffin Ed Johnson. Like the best of Himes's work, his detective fiction constitutes a holler against racism that can still be heard today.

A campus scene at the University of Chicago. In 1948, Himes was invited to speak here on the problems of being a black writer. He maintained in his lecture that the country demanded the truth from a black writer and yet rejected it.

A
Grim
Youth

Chapter Two

A Grim Youth

CHESTER BOMAR HIMES was born on July 29, 1909, in Jefferson City, Missouri. He was the youngest of three boys. Edward was 10 years his senior and Joseph was one year older.

Chester's father, Joseph, was head of the mechanical-arts department at Lincoln Institute, where he taught the crafts of the blacksmith and the wheelwright. His mother, Estelle, was a former teacher. Joseph Himes, Sr., was proud of his dark skin color and the color he saw in his sons, but his wife, who was so light skinned that she could be mistaken for

The youngest of three children, Himes grew up in a well-schooled family. Both his mother and his father worked as teachers.

white, felt strongly that the whiter one was, the better.

When Chester was eight years old, his family moved to Alcorn, Mississippi, where Joseph Himes, Sr., had secured a teaching position at

Alcorn A. & M. College. His mother was appalled at the notion of having to move south to rural, segregated Mississippi, where racism was quite prevalent. Because she thought that the local black schools were not very good, she

Joseph and Estelle Himes moved their family several times while their sons (from left to right) Joseph, Jr., Edward, and Chester were growing up.

taught Joe and Chester at home. (Edward had left home by then to attend college.) When Chester enrolled in public school for the first time, in 1917, he was put into the eighth grade. He and his brother Joe were quite advanced in their studies, and their classmates were often twice their age.

Because Estelle Himes was unhappy in Mississippi, she purposely created a series of scandals in an effort to force the family to move back north. When Himes's father bought a used car, she took her sons for long country rides. One day, she was threatened by an angry farmer who claimed that her car had frightened his mules. She responded by drawing a pistol. This incident was not severe enough to force her husband and family out of the state, as she had planned. However, her next attempt was a success. Taking advantage of her light coloring, she spent a night in a whites-only hotel. The next morning, she loudly proclaimed her racial identity. The ensuing trouble caused the Alcorn College president to dismiss Joseph Himes, Sr. The family soon left Mississippi for good.

In 1921, Chester's father obtained a post at Branch Normal College in Pine Bluff, Arkansas, where in addition to manual trades he taught Negro history. His two youngest sons matriculated at the college as first-year students even though Joseph was only 13 and Chester was only 12. Most of the collegians were in their twenties.

The following year, a turning point took place in the brothers' lives. For a chemistry demonstration at a school assembly, they built a tabletop torpedo fueled with saltpeter, charcoal, and ground glass. Shortly before the demonstration was about to begin, Chester was punished by his mother and was not allowed to participate in the demonstration. Instead, he sat in the auditorium and watched as the torpedo exploded in Joe's face, blinding him.

Joe was rushed to a nearby whites-only hospital, where he was refused admittance. He was then taken to a hospital for blacks. His family was told that nothing could be done to save his sight. Five days later, Estelle Himes took him to Barnes Hospital in St. Louis, Missouri, where she believed his eyesight could be restored. That fall, her husband and Chester followed them to St. Louis.

Unable to find a teaching position in St. Louis, Joseph Himes, Sr., waited tables in a beer hall. Joe, when not undergoing hospital treatment, attended an integrated school for the blind, while Chester entered Wendell Phil-

When Himes was 17 years old, he began to work at the Wade Park Manor, an exclusive hotel in Cleveland, Ohio. After being employed there for only a few weeks, he suffered a crippling accident while he was on the job.

lips High School, a segregated institution.
Feeling guilty about his brother's accident, he
became lonely and sullen. He often cut classes

Himes planned on studying medicine when he entered Ohio State University in 1926. However, he left the school permanently during his freshman year.

and roamed through the unfamiliar city, spending hours at the railroad station watching the trains go by. His feelings of guilt grew even more when little progress was made on Joe's eyes and his doctors declared that nothing more could be done for him.

In 1923, Joseph Himes, Sr., moved his family again, this time to Cleveland, Ohio, where his brother and two married sisters lived. At first, the Himes family lived with these relatives. However, Chester's mother did not get along with them. Even though her husband had helped his relatives move north and become established, they acted condescendingly to him now that he was unemployed. She finally decided to leave the household and took Joe to live in a distant neighborhood. Chester's father eventually found carpentry and small construction work and saved enough money to buy a house in nearby Glenville, a white middle-class neighborhood, where the family was reunited.

Chester enrolled at East High School in Cleveland, where his academic career was anything but excellent. He graduated in January 1926, at the age of 17, by the grace of a clerical error: His grade of 56 in Latin was mistakenly recorded as an 86. He planned to study medicine at Ohio State University in Columbus, Ohio, and took a job as a busboy in a fancy hotel, the Wade Park Manor, to save money to help pay for school.

At the Wade Park Manor, Chester's job was to collect room-service food trays and roll them into a service elevator. One day, while he was talking with two staff women, he stepped through an open elevator door and fell down the shaft onto a solid platform, breaking his teeth, his lower jaw, and his left arm above the wrist. He also fractured his three lowest vertebrae.

As had happened with his brother, Chester was turned away from a whites-only hospital, which claimed that there was no bed for him. They gave him a massive shot of morphine to kill the pain and sent him to a black hospital.

At first, Chester's doctors never expected him to walk again. He was put into a body cast, his mouth was anesthetized, and his teeth were wired together. Recovery was slow, and for a long time afterward he had to wear a torturous and humiliating back brace.

The Ohio State Industrial Commission paid all of Chester's hospital, medical, and dental expenses. When he was released from the hospital, the Industrial Commission agreed to pay him a pension of $75 a month for total disability. The Wade Park Manor said that it would continue his monthly $50 salary if he would sign away his right to sue for negligence.

Chester's father persuaded him to accept

the hotel's offer despite Estelle Himes's objections. She wanted to sue the Wade Park Manor because an investigation had proved the hotel entirely responsible for the accident. She thought her son could win a court decision far more favorable than the mere continuation of his salary. Furious at the settlement, she went to the hotel and accused the management of taking advantage of her son. The hotel promptly stopped the extra payments, and because Chester had already waived his rights there was nothing he could do. With this new disagreement adding to his parents' troubles, they fought viciously all the time. By September 1926, Chester was glad to get away from his family and begin college—a rare opportunity for blacks in the 1920s.

Chester tested with the fourth highest I.Q. in his class at Ohio State University and threw himself into college life. Although state law prohibited racial discrimination, blacks could not live in student dormitories at Ohio State, and the only blacks in nearby fraternities were waiters and dishwashers. Accordingly, Himes rented a room in the city of Columbus from a local black homeowner. With his pension, he bought a coonskin coat, a long-stemmed pipe, and a Ford Model T car. He pledged at Alpha Phi Alpha—one of the college's two black fraternities.

Despite Chester's attempts to enjoy college life, he quickly became depressed by the racism he saw at college and in the city of Columbus. Besides being kept from living in the student dormitories, blacks were not welcome at many Ohio State campus functions. Downtown movie theaters restricted blacks to upper balconies or refused to seat them at all, and restaurants would not serve them. Upset by these restrictions, Chester fared badly in school. After he had a fight with a laboratory instructor, he never returned to class. He received failing grades in all his courses, but he was not dropped from school that semester.

The marital tension at Chester's home during his Christmas vacation was unbearable. His parents quarreled so fiercely that Chester gladly returned to Columbus at the holiday's end. Yet he was increasingly irritated by his properly behaved black classmates, who seemed to imitate the behavior of whites. Consequently, he decided to play a prank on some of them. He convinced six couples to go with him to a quiet house where they could listen to records. However, the couples soon found out that the house was actually a speakeasy, where liquor was served illegally. Deeply offended by Chester's prank, they reported him to the men's dean the next day. He was quickly invited to withdraw from school as a result of "ill health and failing grades."

Chester then returned to his parents' house. Although he was obviously a bright young man, he had become, at the age of 18, a college dropout without any discernible future.

Himes as a teenager, at a time when his family was living in Cleveland, Ohio.

Crime
and
Punishment

Chapter Three

Crime and Punishment

BY THE SUMMER of 1927, Himes had entered a world that was very much removed from academic life. A friend from the Wade Park Manor had introduced him to an illegal gambling club, Bunch Boy's, on Cedar Avenue in Cleveland, where the 18-year-old Himes learned to play blackjack and craps and to bet on horses. Bunch Boy's mainly attracted black servants and laborers rather than professional gamblers or criminals, although Bunch Boy himself had once been kidnapped by gangster Al Capone and ransomed for $80,000. Himes and Bunch Boy became friendly with one

After Himes left college in 1927, he returned to live with his parents in Cleveland, Ohio. Before long, he began to explore life in the city's underworld.

another, and because Himes had a steady income from his Industrial Commission pension, Bunch Boy lent him money so he could play blackjack compulsively. Eventually, Himes helped run the games and learned to drink whiskey, which was outlawed by the federal government during the 1920s.

By the winter, Himes was filling in as a bellhop at the Hotel Gilsy, earning $50 or more a night bringing prostitutes to men's rooms and selling home-brewed alcohol. He used his earnings to shoot dice at Hotstuff's, another gambling club, which attracted more colorful characters than Bunch Boy's. Caught up in a fast and reckless life-style, he bought expensive clothes and a used touring car, which he soon wrecked, driving it into a concrete stanchion. He smoked opium and, with a friend named Benny, he began a career of petty thievery. Himes would take Benny to men's clothing stores and chat with the clerks while Benny stole items such as cigarette lighters and cuff links that were on display. The two were soon stealing cars.

Benny was also responsible for introducing Himes to Jean Johnson. Before long, Himes and his new girlfriend were living together in an apartment behind Bunch Boy's. Prohibition laws had created a lucrative market for illegally brewed alcohol, and Himes and Jean Johnson supported themselves by selling "bootleg" whiskey. However, Benny soon talked Himes into committing a burglary. Having learned of a large supply of weapons and ammunition stored at a nearby YMCA, they planned to steal some automatic pistols and cartridges and sell them to black steelworkers in the nearby Ohio towns of Warren and Youngstown.

The robbery seemed to go smoothly. However, the police trailed the duo to Warren, where they had taken a room, and arrested them. Himes and Benny were returned to Cleveland the next day under police escort.

Himes told his mother he knew nothing of the crime and had only gone along for the ride. Although she did not believe him, she feared sending him to jail and agreed to plead for him at a hearing. She detailed the family's history before a judge, describing Himes's fall down the elevator shaft and his withdrawal from college. She claimed that his father had failed to exercise a proper influence over him, so Himes was easily led astray. The judge found the story extraordinarily moving. Because the guns had been recovered and no actual harm had been done, the judge gave Himes a suspended sentence. Benny was jailed for 30

Federal agents enforce strict Prohibition laws by emptying contraband alcohol into the street. In 1927, Himes attempted to bypass these laws by making and selling his own liquor.

days.

Estelle Himes then sought to control her son's pension and tried to send him to an institution for unmanageable youths. His father refused to send him there; the parental battles worsened. One night Himes heard a loud

commotion in the house and ran downstairs.
His father, who was bleeding from the fore-
head after having been struck by his wife with
a flatiron, had pinned her to a wall and was
choking her. Himes pulled them apart. His
father then packed his bags and left. He never

lived with them again.

The next week, Himes and Benny stole a car and drove to Columbus, where Himes visited some friends at Ohio State. While in a dormitory, he saw a freshman's identity card and impulsively stole it. After substituting his own name on the card, he used the false ID to write bad checks all over the city. In a very short time, he bilked as many as 20 stores. He made small purchases with large checks and received the difference in cash. Finally, a suspicious store clerk tried to verify the ID, and Himes was again caught and arrested. He was locked up until his trial.

This time Himes's father pleaded for him. The judge gave him a two-year suspended sentence and a five-year bench parole, which meant that if he committed any crime—even a misdemeanor— anywhere in Ohio in the next five years, the suspension would be revoked, and he would be returned to Columbus to serve his sentence.

However, Himes's behavior did not improve after his second brush with the law. He continued to stay out at night with Jean Johnson, often at Bunch Boy's. He carried a gun everywhere and would often act extremely violently. One day, when he was refused service at a restaurant counter, he jumped onto it, kicked all of the plates, glasses, pie tins, and cups to the floor, then struck the girl behind the counter and beat the proprietor with his pistol. Himes then walked out of the restaurant without being arrested or charged for a crime.

In November 1928, Himes heard a chauffeur at Bunch Boy's bragging about the large sums of money that his white employers, the Millers, kept in a wall safe at their exclusive Cleveland Heights home. Himes had dreamed of leaving Cleveland and his family and going abroad. However, he lacked the money for such an escape. He imagined his opportunity had arrived when the Millers' chauffeur let slip that neither he nor the Millers would be home on Thanksgiving Eve.

Himes went to look over the house. He asked the maid for the chauffeur, planning on drawing his gun on her and forcing his way in, but she refused to open the door and went to call the police. He hid in the shrubs while the police came and left. After the Millers returned and disappeared into the house, he broke into the garage and followed a passage into the house. He pulled a gun on the Millers, locked the maid in a bathroom, ripped the phone from the wall, and proceeded to loot the house. He then returned to the garage and slipped into one of the Millers' cars. It was snowing heavily and visibility was low as he drove away from the house. Suddenly, shots rang out. When he heard a siren wail, he realized that the police were behind him.

Himes roared off down the road. Before long, the pursuing patrol car had disappeared from view. Snow coated his windshield, so he could barely see the road in front of him. He swerved and crashed through a hedge, and his car became stuck in a snow-covered pasture.

Himes then trudged on foot for hours before arriving at an all-night bar, where he accidentally dropped a diamond ring on the floor. He shakily retrieved it, and the bartender and a half-drunk police officer—the only other customer in the bar—gave him a bit of trouble before dismissing the ring as a worthless fake.

Later on, Himes took a train to Chicago and went to fence the jewelry at a pawnshop he had learned of at Bunch Boy's. The proprietor went into his back room to examine the diamond ring and called the police. Two detectives arrived and searched Himes. They found the rest of the stolen jewelry and took him to the detective bureau, where they interrogated him. Himes claimed that the jewelry was his. They then handcuffed his feet and hands behind his back, hung him upside down on an open door, cushioned their pistols in felt hats, and pistol-whipped him until he confessed.

Himes was returned to Cleveland and put into the Cuyahoga County jail to await sentencing. His grief-stricken mother visited him, while Joseph Himes, Sr., arranged for an attorney for his son. Both of Himes's parents were deeply hurt by his latest act, but Himes refused to acknowledge either their pain or his own. On December 27, 1928, he was sentenced to 20 to 25 years of hard labor in the Ohio State Penitentiary. He was only 19 years old.

During the Prohibition era, passwords and code names were often needed to gain entrance to a speakeasy—an illegal nightclub that served alcohol.

From the Pen

Chapter Four

From the Pen

LIFE IN THE Ohio State Penitentiary proved to be an extension of the sordid life that Himes had recently come to know. He continued to receive his $75 monthly payments from the Industrial Commission, so he never had to work at prison jobs alongside the other convicts. Instead, he occupied himself with gambling, which inside the prison walls determined the power structure among inmates. Himes was soon running the games. His intelligence and schooling helped to keep him on the top of the action because even the most violent criminals seemed awed by his educa-

Prisoners at the Ohio State Penitentiary watch from the safety of the prison yard as fire fighters battle a huge and devastating fire that took the lives of more than 300 men on April 20, 1930. Himes entered the prison in 1928, when he was 19 years old, and was not released until more than seven years later.

tion. Others often intervened to protect him when a fight broke out because he had become indispensable as the person who ran the games and bribed the guards.

During his jail term, Himes took up writing as a way to pass the time. After sending stories to various publishers, he met with success in such black publications as the *Atlanta World*, the *Pittsburgh Courier*, the *Afro-American*, the *Bronzeman*, and *Abbott's Monthly*. Himes's stories were often quite violent, characterized by abrupt shifts of plot, desperate actions, and unexpected consequences. They also reflected his cynical view of human nature. He maintained, "People will do anything—white people, black people, all people." Again and again, Himes wrote about autobiographical incidents. He wrote about his Thanksgiving Eve robbery in "His Last Day," the story of a condemned murderer reexperiencing his life while waiting for the electric chair. "Prison Mass" featured a self-portrait in Brightlights, an inmate who has committed crimes similar to those committed by Himes. Like his author, Brightlights was a budding writer.

Himes also wrote stories with subjects beyond his own experience. "Her Whole Existence: A Story of True Love" was a romantic tale typical of those appearing in women's magazines in the 1930s. "I Don't Want to Die" was a tearjerker in which a dying prisoner envisioned himself leading a law-abiding, middle-class life. "He Knew" was a hard-edged crime story featuring two tough black detectives.

Himes's breakthrough came in 1934, when two stories—"Crazy in the Stir," about an inmate's hysteria, and "To What Red Hell," which told of a prison fire in horrific, almost surrealistic detail—were accepted by *Esquire* magazine, one of the premier magazines for American creative writing. The half dozen of his stories that the magazine published over the subsequent two years were attributed to "Prisoner No. 59623."

Following these publications, Himes's fellow convicts began to respect him even more. Abusive prison guards had to be careful with their anonymous celebrity.

During Himes's term in prison, his father visited him only once—to borrow money. During the economic depression that swept the United States in the 1930s, Himes's disability pension made him the most prosperous member of the family. His mother visited him more frequently. She was living in Columbus with Joe, who was studying for a doctorate in sociology at Himes's alma mater, Ohio State.

To help with his brother's school expenses, Himes assigned his pension to his mother.

Himes was paroled to her in May 1936 after being in prison for more than seven years. *Es-*

quire soon published his last prison story, "Every Opportunity," about an inmate's inability to adjust to life outside prison or to find steady employment in depression America. It

A crowd awaits the opening of an employment office during the Great Depression. Himes was greeted by a lack of job opportunities following his release from prison in 1936.

was prophetic.

A friend introduced Himes to marijuana, and he got so high from the drug that he thought he was having a heart attack and begged to see a doctor. The doctor told Himes's mother the reason for her son's sup-

Grim-faced job applicants compete for a limited number of employment openings with the Cleveland city government during the economic depression of the 1930s. Although Himes was occasionally able to find work during this period, he attempted to earn some additional income through his writings.

posed illness, and in desperation she switched his parole to his father, who was teaching in Cleveland under the auspices of the Works Progress Administration (WPA), a federal agency formed during the Great Depression to provide work for the unemployed. Himes's

parole was supposed to last 17 years, the dura-
tion of his prison term. He could not choose
where to live or work without his probation
officer's permission.

On August 13, 1937, Himes married Jean
Johnson. The couple lived in Cleveland in a
succession of shabby rented rooms. Himes
wanted to support his new wife with his writings and tried, with limited success, to write
for popular magazines. "The Night's for Cry-
in'," set in the black ghetto, was his first story
to be published in *Esquire* that was written
after his parole. "Pork Chop Paradise" told of
an ugly man with a compelling voice who
prayed his way from prison into a career as
a ghetto evangelist, convinced that he was
God. "A Nigger" spoke of a black man living
off his girlfriend, who got her money from an
old white racist.

Himes's literary efforts did not bring in
much money. He took part-time work as a
waiter in a country club and a bellhop in several big hotels. Because he did not want his
wife to work, they did not have very much.

Himes was eventually hired by the WPA,
first to dig sewers and dredge creeks in the
Cleveland suburbs, then to work as a research
assistant in the Cleveland Public Library and
to participate in the WPA's Ohio Writers' Proj-

ect, for which he wrote a history of Cleveland. While on the Ohio Writers' Project, he also wrote a series of short pieces for the Cleveland *Daily News*. N. R. Howard, the editor of the *Daily News*, was familiar with Himes's *Esquire* stories and became a good friend. The two talked about writing and literature, and Howard gave Himes much advice.

When the WPA was abolished in 1943, Himes looked for work in private industry. However, he was not successful at this and attributed his failure to racial prejudice. Desperate to leave Cleveland, he convinced his probation officer to have the governor end his parole and restore his citizenship, which had been automatically revoked when he was imprisoned. He then went to Pleasant Valley, Ohio, to work on Pulitzer Prize winning novelist Louis Bromfield's Malabar Farm.

Bromfield read *Black Sheep*, a novel that Himes had begun writing, and offered to help get it published. But no editor would touch it. Consequently, Himes and his wife took a bus to Los Angeles, California. The celebrated poet Langston Hughes, whom Himes had met in Cleveland shortly after leaving prison, had given Himes a list of people to see for work as a screenwriter in Hollywood. Bromfield also went to Hollywood, where he worked on the screen adaptation of writer Ernest Hemingway's *For Whom the Bell Tolls*. He brought *Black Sheep* with him, hoping to interest a Hollywood producer in the work.

Himes had no luck with Hughes's list or Bromfield's efforts. He discovered that racial prejudice was strong in Los Angeles, where blacks were welcome to work only at menial labor. Even the cast of the 1943 all-black musical *Cabin in the Sky*, which included respected and well-known entertainers Lena Horne, Ethel Waters, Louis Armstrong, and Duke Ellington, was barred from eating in the commissary on the MGM studio lot.

Himes also had no luck when it came to helping the United States in World War II. Called for an army physical in 1943, he was turned down because of his disabilities from his accident in the elevator shaft. Instead, he went to work in the Los Angeles shipyards. He had learned various mechanical skills from his father, and he knew how to read blueprints; do carpentry, plumbing, wiring, and roofing; and operate machine tools. However, blacks were usually considered for unskilled work only, and his stint in the shipyards did not last for long. In a 3-year period, he held 23 jobs.

During this time, Himes published several stories in black venues such as *Opportunity* and *The Crisis*, the magazine published by the National Association for the Advancement of Colored People (NAACP). Some of his stories returned to the earlier prison settings. However, World War II formed the background for "Two Soldiers" and "So Softly Smiling," propagandistic efforts calling for unification in the war effort. Himes hoped that the war against Adolf Hitler's Nazi regime in Germany indicated that America was ready to lay aside its history of racial oppression: If blacks and whites joined together to fight a common enemy, he reasoned, they might realize their common humanity and overcome their racism.

Himes also wrote essays such as "Now Is the Time! Here Is the Place!" and "Negro Martyrs Are Needed," which anticipated the civil rights movement of the 1960s by calling on middle-class blacks to use nonviolent resistance to attract attention to the cause of racial freedom and to rally blacks in the ghetto. In "Democracy Is for the Unafraid," he asked whites to join the struggle and prove that they did not fear equality.

After this brief period of optimism, Himes's experience in the Los Angeles shipyards and rumors of rampant prejudice in the armed forces brought back despair. In 1943, he published "Zoot Riots Are Race Riots," an eye-

witness account of white servicemen in Los
Angeles savagely beating Mexican-Americans
with complete impunity. "Christmas Gift" told
of a much-decorated black serviceman who
returns home from the European front and is

killed by whites on Christmas Eve for no other reason than that he was black and he was back. "One More Way to Die" was the first-person account of a black man helplessly, senselessly murdered by two white California

Louis Bromfield and his wife survey their farm in Pleasant Valley, Ohio. A Pulitzer Prize winning novelist, Bromfield took an interest in Himes's career and hired him as a farmhand in 1943.

policemen. "All God's Chillun Got Pride," an autobiographical piece about the racism to which Himes was subjected in the Cleveland Public Library, was published in 1944.

Throughout this period, Himes worked days as a laborer, mostly shoveling gravel and sand or moving mountains of paper. Meanwhile, his wife had gotten a much better job. She was codirector of women's activities for the Los Angeles area USOs (servicemen's organizations). Himes resented her position and the respect she received from her white co-workers, and this put a tremendous strain on their marriage. Jean did not mind being responsible for their livelihood, which only hurt him more.

This pain and frustration, fused with his shipyard experience, led to his second attempt at a novel, *If He Hollers Let Him Go*, in which the protagonist, Bob Jones, like Himes, comes to Los Angeles from Cleveland, hoping to be freed from racial self- consciousness. Throughout the book, Jones suffers racially oriented anxiety dreams, which are reflected in reality: A white woman worker refuses to work under him; a foreman takes the woman's side and demotes Jones; a light-skinned girlfriend argues that whites are really trying to help black people; and a false accusation of attempted rape results in his being knocked out with a hammer and marched off to enlist in the war against fascism overseas.

In 1944, Himes's literary efforts helped him to win a fellowship from the Julius Rosenwald Foundation in Chicago to finish this bitter protest novel. Later in the year, *If He Hollers Let Him Go* was accepted by a New York publisher. After so much hardship, his luck seemed to be changing.

One of America's leading black poets, Langston Hughes (shown here) befriended Himes in Cleveland, Ohio, as he was embarking on a career as a novelist. Hughes sought to help Himes find employment when the aspiring writer moved to California in 1943.

A
Lonely
Crusade

Chapter Five

A Lonely Crusade

Himes's first novel, *If He Hollers Let Him Go*, was published in 1944 to mostly excellent reviews. Some readers objected to the abrupt and melodramatic plot twists, the book's bitter tone, and its general unpleasantness. Yet Richard Wright's powerful and violent novel *Native Son*, published in 1940, had helped to pave the way for Himes. Himes's book was nominated for the George Washington Carver Award—sponsored by his publisher, Doubleday—and a $2,500 prize. Himes was enraged when it lost to *Mrs. Palmer's Honey*, a novel about a black maid written by a white

The shipyards of Los Angeles, California, were a center of activity in the early 1940s as the shipbuilding industry geared up for World War II. The racism that Himes encountered while working in these shipyards became part of Lonely Crusade, *his second novel.*

woman, Fannie Cook. His publisher advertised the winning novel by contrasting it with an unnamed novel, clearly *If He Hollers Let Him Go*, which it called "a series of epithets punctuated by spit."

Critics castigated Himes for his use of objectionable language and his failure to offer a solution to the racial problems he exposed in his novel. In a feature in the magazine *Saturday Review*, Himes answered that if the powerful U.S. government, which had demonstrated incredible resolve and ability during World War II, could not provide an answer to the "Negro problem," how could Himes, a mere writer, be expected to do so?

Thoroughly unhappy with how his publisher had treated him, Himes, who had come to New York for the publication of his first novel, switched to another publisher for his next book. He did so at the suggestion of Carl Van Vechten, an influential writer and advocate of black artists whom Himes had met through author Richard Wright, a recent acquaintance. Both Wright and Van Vechten would remain among Himes's closest friends.

Alfred A. Knopf Publishers agreed to publish Himes's second novel, *Lonely Crusade*, and he returned to California to work on the book. Driving west, he and his wife encountered an alarming amount of racial prejudice. They were refused service in hotels, motels, and restaurants. Frightened by the abuse they met and by rumors of recent agitation in northern California by the white supremacist group the Ku Klux Klan, they traveled with a loaded rifle by their side after they passed through Illinois.

Himes and Jean moved into a dilapidated three-room shack on Jean's brother's ranch at Honey Lake, in northern California. Sand lizards crawled over the floor, and field rats gnawed in the walls all night. While battling lizards, rats, and rattlesnakes, Himes finished the first draft of his novel. In *Lonely Crusade*, he created a new alter ego, Lee Gordon, an educated black in wartime Los Angeles who cannot get a decent job. Plagued by self-hatred and anger at white society, he finally accepts a position as a union organizer and is caught up in a battle between numerous forces—factory management, the Communist party, police, unions, blacks, whites.

Himes finished the draft of his book, spent a restful summer in California, and then returned with Jean to New York. He became the caretaker of a Long Island estate, where he had few responsibilities and few visitors, except for such friends as Ralph Ellison, who was then writing what would be a major novel on black life in America, *Invisible Man*, published in 1952. There was plenty of quiet and free time in which to finish revising *Lonely Crusade*.

In 1947, the couple moved to Harlem's Theresa Hotel, and then to a private apartment.

After the publication of Himes's first novel, If He Hollers Let Him Go, in 1945, he found himself in the spotlight of the publishing world. He is shown here with (from left to right) his wife, Jean; Professor Sterling Brown; and author Bucklin Moor.

Jean began to work as a recreational director at a girls' camp for juvenile delinquents on Welfare Island. Knopf, which was about to publish *Lonely Crusade*, offered Himes a $2,000 advance for a book on his experiences in Hollywood. It would be called *Immortal Mammy*. The future continued to look promis-

ing.

Despite fears of a libel suit because Himes's portrayal of one industrialist was frighteningly realistic, Knopf heavily publicized *Lonely Crusade*'s release on October 8, 1947. They scheduled Himes to speak on several radio programs and to make appearances at Macy's and Bloomingdale's, major New York department stores.

When Himes went to Macy's, he found that the head of the book department had canceled the scheduled talk. At Bloomingdale's, he could not find any copies of his book on display. The salesclerk had not heard of him, and the manager of the book department would not see him. Dazed, Himes called Jean to arrange to meet for his appearance on the popular Mary Margaret McBride radio show and learned that his appearance had been canceled. Later on, he was dropped from a CBS radio network broadcast.

Lonely Crusade proved to be an apt title; Himes was attacked from all sides once the book was published. The Communist party was particularly vicious, printing a cartoon in the *Daily Worker* depicting him as a black

One of Harlem's most noted hotels, the Theresa, did not admit blacks until around 1940, when it quickly became a central meeting place for blacks.

man marching with a white flag. Himes felt black critics were antagonistic because he was claiming that centuries of oppression meant extra efforts were necessary to produce more than superficial equality. They had mistaken his call for special privileges as a confession of blacks' inferiority.

Utterly discouraged, Himes yearned to leave the United States. He took any job he could get while his wife worked as a recreational director for housing projects in New York. They lived in a rented room in the Bronx, New York, and Jean's better position once again increased the strain on their marriage.

Himes proceeded to work on *Black Sheep* and cut it to half its original length. He was then invited to the artists' retreat at Yaddo, where all he accomplished was a short story about a writer-in-residence at an artists' retreat who drunkenly tries and fails to write a novel entitled *I Was Looking for a Street*.

After Himes stayed at Yaddo and gave a speech on "The Dilemma of the Negro Writer" at the University of Chicago, he returned to New York. For the next year, he worked as a bellhop and then as a caretaker in various resorts in New York and New Jersey. He tried unsuccessfully to adapt his first novel, *If He Hollers Let Him Go*, into a stage play.

In the summer of 1949, he and his wife bought a used car and moved to a rented room in Bridgeport, Connecticut, where Himes thought he would be able to write in peace.

The idyll was brief. By mid-July, their money was gone. After deciding to move back to New York, where Jean expected a job with the Welfare Department, Himes placed a classified ad in a local paper, offering to sell his car for $100. Jean took all but 50 cents of the remaining money to go to New York to apply for her job. Himes remained in Connecticut to sell the car. A young black factory worker offered to buy it, promising to return later in the day with the cash. Himes decided to drive the car one last time and buy himself a pack of cigarettes. When he pulled out of his parking space, his sedan's front bumper tore the fender off a new car being driven the wrong way on a one-way street by a well-dressed white woman. Himes smelled liquor on her breath and thought the cause of the minor accident was obvious.

When the police arrived, the woman told them that the accident was Himes's fault. He was promptly arrested for reckless driving. His bail was set at $25, yet he had no money with him. He told the desk sergeant that he was a well-known writer and politely asked to

be released on his own recognizance. The desk
sergeant claimed that the law did not permit
him to do so. Instead, Himes would be allowed
to call his wife at 8:00, when he expected her
back from New York. However, the guard on

Author Richard Wright (left) and his wife, Ellen, with actor Lionel Stander at a Harlem cafe. Although Wright became celebrated in the United States after his novel Native Son *was published in 1940, he eventually left America to live in France. In the early 1950s, Himes would become an expatriate writer as well.*

the evening shift was not properly notified, and he would not let Himes make his phone call. Himes had to spend the night in jail.

The next morning, his hearing was postponed a week because the other driver was unable to appear in court. It was 11:00 A.M. before Himes telephoned his wife, who had stayed in New York overnight. She was just rushing into their rented room in Connecticut

to answer the phone when Himes hung up. Beginning to worry, she called several local hospitals, thinking that Himes might have been in an accident. It was a long time before

The Skyline Room at the Theresa Hotel in Harlem, where Himes often stayed during his visits to New York.

she thought to call the police.

Unable to reach Jean, Himes called her brother in Baltimore, Maryland, who agreed to wire $100. Then Himes was taken to the county prison, where he was photographed, fingerprinted, and issued a numbered uniform. It was a nightmare, reminiscent of the day 21 years before when he had been sent to the Ohio State Penitentiary for armed robbery.

When Jean finally found her husband, she did not have the money to bail him out. Nor could she visit him because it was Wednesday, and visits were only allowed on Tuesdays and Thursdays. Back home, she received a telegram from her brother telling of the $100. She rushed to the jail, where she learned that the money had been returned to the telegraph office because prisoners could not receive wired money. At the telegraph office, she could not get the money because the wire was addressed to her husband. She could only have the money if Himes and the prison warden signed an authorization. When the warden insisted that this was illegal, it began to seem that the celebrated novelist would be imprisoned indefinitely.

Jean cried until the warden agreed to break the rules. The authorization was signed, the money was retrieved, and Himes was bailed out of jail. When he got back to his car, he found a traffic violation for parking illegally overnight. The factory worker soon appeared and gave Himes only $75 for the car because of the damage that had been done in the accident.

The following morning, Himes and his wife boarded a train for New York. Himes's encounter with the law had rattled his nerves. He was not surprised; he had come to expect disasters. But the jailing had stirred up anxieties he had long sought to suppress. He resolved yet again to leave the United States. He would go to Europe as soon as he could, if he ever had enough money.

Himes spent most of his time in New York drinking so heavily that he suffered blackouts and was unable to remember anything. The only work he took was a weeklong stint as a doorman in Long Beach, New York. When Richard Wright returned from a year in France, he helped Himes get a loan of $500.

More work as a caretaker on a farm near Stamford, Connecticut, allowed Himes to complete *Black Sheep*, which recounted the story of his 1928 robbery in Cleveland and described prison life in great detail. The book chronicled the incarceration of Jim Monroe, who runs the gambling games and begins to write while in

Among Himes's friends in the literary world was Ralph Ellison, whose powerful novel Invisible Man *examines the lack of visibility of blacks in American society.*

prison. Reverting to a strategy he had used with *Esquire* in the 1930s, Himes changed the major characters into white men. At a party in New York, he met Bill Raney, an editor who encouraged Himes to submit the book to him.

In June 1950, Himes went to Durham, North Carolina, to teach a two-week seminar in creative writing at North Carolina College, a job arranged by his brother Joe, who had become a professor of sociology at the college. There Himes received a letter from Bill Raney indicating—or so he thought—that *Black Sheep* had been accepted.

Himes returned to New York and threw a celebratory party at the Theresa Hotel for friends. When he went to Raney's office the next day, expecting to sign a contract and pick up his advance payment, he found his manuscript tied up in a neat package. A managing editor had backed down from taking it. After paying his hotel bill, Himes had $12 left.

Himes and his wife then went to Westlake, Vermont, to live with Bill Smith, a writer they had known in California, until they could support themselves again. Finally, Jean got a position as recreational director of the Women's Reformatory in Mount Kisco, New York. Himes sought a position on the editorial staff of *Reader's Digest* in nearby Pleasantville, but

he ended up typing metal stencils for the ad-
dressograph machines and left after one day.
He spent the next three months as a porter
and janitor at the YMCA in White Plains, New
York, then moved back to Harlem alone, convinced that he was a failure as a writer and
a husband. By this time, his strained marriage
was coming to an end. Jean refused to visit
or support him any longer.

Himes isolated himself, unwilling even to see
Langston Hughes or Ralph Ellison. Richard
Wright had moved to France, and Himes felt
strangely distanced from his other friends in
the New York publishing world. He began to
look inward instead and started to write his
most thoroughly autobiographical novel, *The
Third Generation*. The Thomas family in his
novel matched his own, from the mother's
obsession with whiteness, to the blinding ex-
plosives experiment, to the elevator accident,
to one son's college, gambling, and amatory
adventures and his life of crime. Only the
melodramatic ending, in which the father is
stabbed to death, deviated from the details of
Himes's own life.

Both *The Third Generation* and *Black Sheep*
passed from publisher to publisher. Himes was
working a hotel switchboard in 1951 when he
received a telegram informing him that *The*

Third Generation had been accepted by World Publishing Company.

Elated, he picked up his advance payment and felt an urge to celebrate. He thought immediately of Vandi Haygood, the former director of fellowships for the Rosenwald Foundation, with whom he had spent a weekend in Chicago many years before. He now went to see her in New York, and they began a tormented affair. For the next year and a half, Himes and Haygood carried on a relationship fraught with violence and drug and alcohol abuse. Eventually, Himes began to experience extended blackouts. By Christmas 1952, he had exhausted his advance.

Himes then went north to Vermont to spend the winter with Bill Smith. He soon learned that *Black Sheep*, retitled *Cast the First Stone*, had been accepted for publication and that he was due a sizable advance. He decided at last to go to Europe. He had many friends among the expatriate American blacks living in Paris, including Richard Wright, who enthusiastically encouraged him to join them. In addition, French critics had cited the translation of *Lonely Crusade* as one of the five best American books published in France in 1952, along with works by Herman Wouk, Ernest Hemingway, F. Scott Fitzgerald, and William Faulkner, an author Himes especially admired.

Himes and Haygood made plans to meet in Paris. He then booked passage for April 1953 on an ocean liner. Twenty-five years after he had first dreamed of going abroad, Himes set sail for Europe aboard the *Ile de France*.

Himes was also greatly influenced by the writings of William Faulkner (shown here), whose novels, set in the South, often depicted a decaying society. One of America's most celebrated authors, Faulkner won the Nobel Prize for Literature in 1949 and the Pulitzer Prize for fiction in 1954 and 1962.

On
the Run

Chapter Six

On
the Run

O N HIMES'S THIRD day at sea, he was wandering down a passageway when he saw a woman pressed up against the wall, seemingly paralyzed. He instinctively moved to help her. She threw her arms around him and clung to him, begging him not to leave her; she then abruptly let go and apologized. Blushing, she introduced herself as Alva Trent Van Olden Barneveldt. She suffered from claustrophobia, a fear of enclosed spaces, she explained. The long, narrow corridor, with its rows of locked doors, had caused a momentary panic.

Himes helped the woman to her cabin and

When Himes arrived in Paris, France, in 1953, he discovered that the city was home to a group of American expatriates—writers, artists, and musicians who felt alienated by their homeland.

left her there. Later that day, he met her again on the ship's deck. They began to talk and they were soon spending all of their time together. Himes learned of Trent's marriage to a Dutchman, his collaboration with the Nazis, and her own heroic efforts for the Allies during World War II. He also learned of their several separations and her nervous breakdowns. She had been living with an aunt in Philadelphia, Pennsylvania, for the past two years and was now returning to Holland to arrange for a divorce, despite her fears of life at 40 without her children or money. Before long, she was promising to join Himes in France after obtaining her divorce.

Himes arrived in Paris on April 11, 1953. Richard Wright helped him find a room across from the Cafe Tournon, a hangout for black expatriate artists and writers. Through Wright, Himes met many black American artists in exile, including the writer James Baldwin, author of *Go Tell It on the Mountain*.

After Himes's first week in Paris, Vandi Haygood appeared. Despite the violence that had characterized their affair in the United States, they spent a pleasant week together. When she left for Madrid, Himes went to search for a decent hotel for Trent. On the day of her arrival, he found a cheap hotel near the

Luxembourg Gardens.

When Yves Malartic, the French translator of *Lonely Crusade,* offered Himes and Trent his villa in Arcachon, on the Bay of Biscay, they left Paris. The endless talk of misfortune among the expatriate blacks in Paris, who seemed to brag of their poor upbringings, unhappy childhoods, and racial sufferings, embarrassed Himes, and he was glad to get away. In contrast, the villagers of Arcachon were good to them, and they lived a quiet life there. Himes rewrote the last chapter of *The Third Generation,* and Trent showed him notes on her life story. He agreed that the story might make a good novel and offered to help her with the writing. They spent two happy months in Arcachon. In July 1953, they moved to London.

By the age of 43, Himes had learned to expect trouble, so he was far from surprised when he discovered upon arriving in London that their passports and money had been stolen. They had traveler's checks, but without passports to identify themselves, they could not cash the checks. A comedy of errors ensued, and Himes spent most of the night going from one police station to the next. When he and Trent eventually reached a hotel, they were met by a night porter who turned away

Among the writers who were living in Paris when Himes settled there in 1953 was James Baldwin (shown here), whose fiction presented a bitter perspective on American race relations.

the interracial couple. Himes and Trent dragged their luggage to another hotel, where they were finally given a room.

The next morning, Himes contacted the American embassy to report the theft of their passports. He called his London publisher, who advanced him some money and issued him a signed letter for identification purposes, and the couple went to the American Express office to cash some traveler's checks. They then went to register with a rental agency to find more permanent living quarters. Many of the apartment listings specified "No Coloreds," so Trent explained to a landlady in London's Randolph Crescent that Himes was merely suntanned. Skeptical, the woman offered them a four-room apartment in her basement.

The American embassy called one morning with the news that the two passports had been found on a bench in Hyde Park. However, the money was gone. Meanwhile, Himes's landlady had realized the truth behind Himes's "suntan" and tried to force him and Trent to move.

The couple moved into an apartment in Hampstead, where they enjoyed the great lawns of Hampstead Heath, the Belsize public library—which Himes was pleased to find had copies of his novels *If He Hollers Let Him Go* and *Lonely Crusade*—and London's abundant nightlife. They worked on Trent's autobiographical novel, *The Golden Chalice*, and finished a draft by mid-December.

When Himes ran low on money, he got a small advance from a British agent who wanted to represent *The Golden Chalice* without having read it. When the agent demanded that Himes do a lot of rewriting before he would show *The Golden Chalice* to some publishers, Himes submitted the draft to his publisher in New York for a small advance. His publisher later rejected the actual manuscript. Dejected and feeling the chill of the oncoming London winter, Himes left with Trent for Majorca, an island off the coast of Spain. On February 1, 1954, they moved into a small house in Puerto de Pollensa.

Ever since the rejection of *The Golden Chalice*, Trent had been quiet and withdrawn. She now abandoned her manuscript completely and occupied herself with household chores. Himes began to work on *The End of a Primitive*, a novel based on his affair with Vandi Haygood. However, his money was dwindling. He continued to receive small advances, including $800 for a book of early short stories about to be published, *Black Boogie Woogie*, and he borrowed money wired from his brother Edward, who was living in Harlem.

Himes's travels in Europe took him to London, England, in 1953. Although the city was noted for being less hostile to blacks than most of urban America, Himes still encountered racial discrimination while he was there and left after half a year.

Himes and Trent next moved to the tiny village of Deya, where Himes quickly settled into a routine, rising early in the morning to begin typing. He said, "I wrote slowly, savoring each word, sometimes taking an hour to fashion one sentence to my liking....That was the first time in my life I enjoyed writing."

In July 1954, Himes completed a draft of his book, submitted it to his publisher in New York, and quickly received a rejection. He and Trent then concentrated on reworking their manuscripts. Next, a French publisher rejected *The End of a Primitive*.

When the stories selected for *Black Boogie Woogie* arrived, Himes read them over again and felt that they were not very good. Publishers had turned down *The Golden Chalice* and *The End of a Primitive*, preferring instead to publish stories that Himes considered to be trash. He wrapped up the stories and hurled them into the sea.

After stopping briefly in Arcachon, the couple returned to Paris, where Himes soon became anxious to return a homesick Trent to her family in Philadelphia. He told her it would not be a separation but an opportunity for her to sell *The Golden Chalice* in New York. After she left, Himes went to London, where he soon received letter after letter from Trent. She was working as a doctor's receptionist in Philadelphia, and in her spare time she was constantly retyping and resubmitting copies of *The Golden Chalice* to editors in New York. She missed Himes terribly, she said. Although Himes was convinced that their love affair would not last in America, he felt unable to remain apart from Trent and left for New York in January 1955.

Himes found a room in Greenwich Village in New York. Trent visited him there on weekends. However, the idyllic existence they had shared abroad was shattered by the harsh reality of racism at home. "We had each," he said, "from the first contact with America, gone back into our separate races."

Himes tried to contact Vandi Haygood and learned that she had died suddenly, at the age of 39. Her abuse of barbiturates was the probable cause of death. He, too, had been using barbiturates since his affair with Haygood. Her death affected him deeply and he abandoned the drug immediately.

While Himes attempted to rework his latest novel, now called simply *The Primitive*, he concentrated on writing short stories. He produced "Boomerang" and "A Little Seed," about Trent's married life; "Spanish Gin," about a party in Puerto de Pollensa, Majorca;

Parisian cafes—including the one shown here—have long been a favorite meeting place of American expatriates. Himes often spent an entire day sitting at a cafe table, discussing current issues with his friends or working on his writing.

"One Night in New Jersey," about life as a caretaker; and "Daydream," based on a Mississippi racial incident. Because *Esquire* had recently bought his story "The Snake," about his 1945 confrontation with a rattler in northern California, he submitted his new stories to the magazine.

Esquire held Himes's new stories for months. Desperate for money, he went to the publisher, Arnold Gingrich, who had been responsible for Himes's first national publication, and demanded to know why he had had no response to his stories, why no stories of his had ever been printed in an *Esquire* anthology, and why *Esquire* had not run a review of *If He Hollers Let Him Go*, particularly when their reviewer, Nobel Prize winner Sinclair Lewis, had been given the book and had promised to review it. Gingrich was embarrassed and apologetic. He had not seen the stories, and his secretary could not find them. He told Himes that he would see to it that the stories were located. Much later, the stories were returned to Himes, unpublished.

Himes went back to menial labor, washing dishes and mopping floors for Horn-Hardart Automats. A lawyer from Legal Aid called Berkeley Books, which had bought the paperback rights to *If He Hollers Let Him Go*, and

Himes's long-delayed payment was immediately forwarded. He then booked passage to Europe for December 14.

Back in Paris, Himes began a new novel, *Mamie Mason*. It was a sexual farce that mocked American liberal sentiment in the 1940s. Whites discover that there are advantages to being black, and as various experts argue that there is no difference between the races, the story turns into a boisterous satire that is in truth a vicious attack on the social inequities that Himes so despised. However, he was unable to sell the incomplete book to French publishers, and he finally put it aside. It would not be published until 1961.

Himes began to feel stifled by his writing and searched his mind for a new direction. He said:

> I had the creative urge, but the old, used forms for the black American writer did not fit my creations. I wanted to break through the barrier that labeled me as a "protest writer." I knew the life of an American black needed another image than just the victim of racism. We were more than just victims. We did not suffer, we were extroverts. We were unique individuals, funny but not clowns, solemn but not serious, hurt but not suffering...we had a tremendous love of life.

Writing was difficult, and Himes's life became a routine of eating, trying to write, and spending drunken evenings at the Cafe Tournon. The cafe had become a famous meeting place for American intellectuals, and Himes and his

A worker stocks an automat machine in a self-service cafeteria. While working at a New York City automat in 1955, Himes witnessed an incident that he later incorporated in one of his detective stories.

friends held court there every night.

When copies of *The Primitive*, which Himes had finally sold to a publisher, arrived from

America and caused a stir at the Cafe Tournon, he became a minor celebrity. People came to the cafe to meet him and to observe the antics of his group of friends. He also began another tortured affair, this time with a very young, emotionally needy German woman named Marlene Behrens who was studying acting in Paris. They moved in and out of various hotels together, continually pawning possessions, starving when their money ran out. They settled longest at the Hotel Rachou, which had become a well-known hangout for American "beatniks," the nonconformists of the 1950s.

Although many of Himes's black friends were involved with white women at the time, they disapproved of his relationship with Behrens. Richard Wright called her a "nothing girl"; she was unsophisticated and aggressive. Himes often wondered why he was involved with her. When he tried to break off their relationship, Behrens panicked and swallowed a bottle of sleeping pills. After she survived, Himes promised to become her fiance. They went to Germany so that he could meet her family. When her father asked the couple to separate for a year, saying that after that time they could marry with his blessing if they

Chapter Seven

Detective Work

ALTHOUGH HIMES'S REPUTATION as a writer was growing in Europe, he had very little money. In late 1955, he took the incomplete *Mamie Mason* to a French publisher, Gallimard, and accidentally ran into Marcel Duhamel, the French translator of *If He Hollers Let Him Go*. Duhamel was now the director of Gallimard's successful detective story series, La Serie Noire.

Duhamel asked Himes to write a story along these lines. Himes's terse, violent, action-packed style would be perfect for detective fiction, Duhamel told him, convincing a reluctant

By the late 1950s, the main thoroughfare in Paris—the Champs Elysees (shown here)—had become quite familiar to the expatriate Himes.

Himes to read a few stories by American authors Raymond Chandler and Dashiell Hammett to get an idea of the genre. The formula was an easy one: Concentrate on action, make the scenes as visual as possible, and avoid long explanations of the characters' psychological motivations—describe what the characters are doing rather than what they are thinking. Do not worry about making sense of the plot until the end.

Himes searched for an excuse to decline Duhamel's offer. When he said that he had no paper, Duhamel reached into his pocket and handed him the equivalent of $125 in French francs. Himes asked for a real advance, and Duhamel offered $1,000. Himes could not resist that much money.

Himes wrote a draft about an old confidence game in which a person is convinced that a "scientist" can change $10 bills into $100 bills and provides a large sum of money in $10 denominations only to be cheated out of it. Himes wove this game into a Harlem story involving twin brothers, one conscientious and hardworking, the other prone to begging in the streets in a nun's habit. The brothers were known as the Gold Dust Twins, and Himes wrote 80 pages about their criminal misadventures. Doubting the value of his effort, he showed the draft to Duhamel, who was pleased but advised him that a crime story needed police.

Himes then invented a pair of black detectives, Grave Digger Jones and Coffin Ed Johnson, unsubtle but intelligent men who want desperately to help their people and believe the law can be maintained only through the use of force. Tough and violent, these detectives are well known throughout Harlem. Using stool pigeons and vicious interrogation techniques, they help not so much to keep peace—an impossibility in Himes's Harlem—but to obtain justice within or without the law.

Himes believed that he had written just what Duhamel wanted in this story, called *The Five-Cornered Square* (subsequently published in America as *For Love of Imabelle* and *A Rage in Harlem*). He reasoned that he was only writing for the French, who would believe anything about Americans. In addition, Duhamel had been right: The detective novel was perfectly suited to the abruptness, violence, and melodrama that had been considered failings in Himes's earlier writing, and the setup of black detectives supervised by white senior officers in Harlem allowed him to explore racial inequities in the guise of entertainment. Through his powerful black detectives, Himes

Detective story writer Dashiell Hammett learned about his subject while working for the Pinkerton detective agency. He became one of the masters of American detective stories in the late 1920s, producing popular works such as The Maltese Falcon.

could redress grievances where before he had been helpless.

Himes finished the story in January 1957. Duhamel asked him what a five-cornered square was, and Himes explained that he had made it up to mean a man so "square" he had more than four corners. Gallimard accepted the manuscript and commissioned Himes to write eight more detective stories.

Himes enjoyed his restored fame among his literary friends, who were especially impressed that he had broken the color barrier to become the first black to write for La Serie Noire. He set his next story in Harlem as well. *A Jealous Man Can't Win* (entitled *The Crazy Kill* when published in the United States) began with a preacher falling out a window during a wake and landing unhurt in a basket of bread. Duhamel was pleased with the outline and advanced more money. Himes was not sure if he could keep to the pace of his contract, which called for a novel every two months, but he was enormously happy writing his violent, absurd stories. Although he felt a bit guilty portraying a Harlem he knew only slightly, feeling as much a tourist as a white man would be, he reasoned that "the Harlem of my books was never meant to be real; I never called it real; I just wanted to take it away from the white man if only in my books."

Himes finished his new book by the beginning of May, and in July he set off with Behrens, who had returned to Paris, for Stuttgart, Germany, to visit Behrens's parents. He felt free for the first time in his life. He did not need to think about America or any of the old problems that had formerly obsessed him. "Now I was a French writer," he wrote proudly, happy to be no longer dependent on the United States.

After visiting Behrens's parents—still displeased with their daughter's choice in men but somewhat appeased by Himes's growing success—the couple stayed with a friend in Copenhagen, Denmark, then rented a small house in nearby Horsholm. Inspired by a line from a song by blues singer Bessie Smith, "If trouble was money I'd be a millionaire," Himes began a new book, *If Trouble Was Money* (subsequently called *The Real Cool Killers*). He wrote 10 pages a day, and when the book was finished in mid-September, he and Behrens returned to Paris, where *The Five-Cornered Square* had become legend. The multitalented Jean Cocteau gave it high praise in a jacket blurb, and author Jean Giono had written, "I give you all of Hemingway, Dos Passos and Fitzgerald for this Chester Himes."

Himes then took Behrens to Majorca, where he planned to write his next book, *It Rained Five Days*, about Alva Trent. He took his title from the lyrics of another blues song.

One of the greatest writers of detective stories, Raymond Chandler published his first novel, The Big Sleep, *in 1939. He went on to write many more stories involving his fictional detective, Philip Marlowe.*

Himes was well aware of the irony of first living in Spain with Trent and writing about Haygood, then living there with Behrens and writing about Trent. The couple soon ran out of money and got more help from Duhamel, but by the time he went back to Paris in late April 1958, he had not accomplished any writing in Spain.

Duhamel was disappointed and suggested that Himes try a book about blacks without his two detectives. Himes spent the summer with Behrens in Vence, in the south of France, writing *Run, Man, Run*, turning the story of a drunken white detective who had waved his pistol in the New York automat where Himes had once worked into a harrowing tale of an actual murder. Refreshed, he returned again to his detective team for *The Big Gold Dream*, a story about the violent search for a huge sum of money that a black maid has won playing an illegal numbers game.

The couple visited Paris only once, when Himes received La Grand Prix du Roman Policier for *The Five-Cornered Square*, named the best detective novel of 1957. Himes was written up in newspapers and photographed. He became very popular in Vence and felt he could live there forever. However, when Behrens's mother appeared and insisted that her daughter return to Germany to finish her education, Himes returned to Paris, alone.

Arriving there at 4:00 A.M., Himes knocked at his friend Lesley Packard's door and asked if he could sleep on her sofa. Packard was an Irish-English librarian, the author of a column for the Paris edition of the New York *Herald Tribune*, whom he had met on one of his stays in Paris. The next morning, he went to the Cafe Tournon, where he was greeted as a celebrity. As he walked around the city, people congratulated him on his success and asked him to autograph copies of *The Five-Cornered Square*. When Himes took Packard out to dinner that night, people stared—not because he was black and she was white but because he had received much publicity in Paris and was well known.

Himes and Packard were soon spending time together whenever they could. He sold Duhamel the notion for a new book, *Don't Play with Death*, and moved into an apartment that Packard helped to find. At the end of June, he drove to Hamburg, Germany, to visit Behrens and to meet with a literary agent who was making plans to publish some of his books in German. When Himes returned to Paris, he worked hard at another book, dubbed *All Shot Up* by his German agent, about a corrupt

Poet, novelist, playwright, and artist Jean Cocteau was one of the most creative minds of 20th-century France. His high praise for Himes's The Five-Cornered Square *was echoed when the book was named in France as the best detective novel of 1957.*

Harlem politician who arranges to steal cam-
paign funds by having himself robbed in public,
only to end up seriously wounded, with no idea
what happened to the money.

Despite Himes's popularity in France, his
work was still not being well received in America. In September 1959, the *New York Times*
printed an article on him that began:

> Himes is a small man with a little mustache
> and a big dog who has written such unsuc-
> cessful books as *The Primitive, Cast the
> First Stone, If He Hollers Let Him Go*, and
> *The Third Generation* and is now writing
> detective stories for the French Saerie
> Noire.

Angered by this latest slight, Himes wrote to
Carl Van Vechten, "I dread reading any refer-
ence to me in the American press; there seems
to be so much calculated ill-will it leaves me
depressed."

When Behrens returned to Paris around
Christmas 1959, she and Himes quarreled constantly. After one fight, she slashed her wrists
with a razor. Himes called the police, who took
her away to an American hospital. Later on,
she was put into a psychiatric hospital in Vin-

cennes, France. She wrote to Himes every day, and he visited her whenever he could. Her father wrote to Himes, begging him to give up his daughter, who was placed in a convalescent home in Germany.

In the meantime, Himes finished *All Shot Up* and began another book, *Be Calm*—later called *The Heat's On*—about gangsters, smuggled drugs, and characters such as Sister Heavenly, Uncle Saint, and Pinky. His detective novels began appearing in paperback in the United States, but he rarely knew which companies published them, and he received little or no money for the rights. The stories were mangled by American editors, which confirmed Himes's feeling that publishing was a nasty business—and which like all such businesses took advantage of blacks.

Himes finally moved in with Packard. When Behrens came back to Paris, Packard told her that Himes had gone south, which he promptly did. He spent the spring driving back and forth to Paris, secretly seeing Packard and accomplishing no work. Near the end of June, he finally went to see Behrens in Munich, Germany. When he returned to Paris, he became engaged to Packard, and they drove to Salerno, Italy, where they took a house.

In November 1960, they heard that Richard

Wright had died suddenly. They rushed home to Paris, where they found Wright's American friends gathered at the Cafe Tournon. Himes had had a falling-out with Wright in 1957. Nevertheless, Wright's death shocked and distressed him. As with Haygood's death, Wright's death upset him deeply. He said:

> It seemed as if Dick's death put an accelerator on my own life, which began to spin like a buzz saw. I wanted to do something quick but I didn't know what. My brain seemed to whirl without purpose. I had never realized before how much influence Dick had over me.

Himes no longer felt like writing, and he spent his time visiting friends and traveling. Duhamel told him that artist Pablo Picasso was thinking of drawing a comic strip based on *The Five-Cornered Square* and took Himes to meet Picasso at his chateau near Cannes, France. However, nothing ever came of the comic strip idea.

Himes next tried his hand at screenwriting. A film had been made of Lorraine Hansberry's 1959 play *A Raisin in the Sun*, a family drama set in Harlem. A number of producers came to Himes, convinced that he could do a better screenplay about family life in Harlem. He then wrote *Baby Sister*, a story about a battle over a 17-year-old girl by three men.

Himes meant for his screenplay to show the stark reality of life in Harlem—the overwhelm-

Pablo Picasso (shown here with his wife) was perhaps the most influential artist of the 20th century. Himes visited the Spanish master in 1960 when he was considering drawing a comic strip based on the characters in Himes's The Five-Cornered Square.

ing feeling of despair that he saw in the lives of black Americans. "When I wrote the last line I began crying and couldn't stop," he maintained. "It was the saddest play ever writ-

ten...it was a Greek tragedy in blackface."

Himes wrote the screenplay quickly, but despite its strong screen potential, it was never filmed. Meanwhile, *Mamie Mason* had been published in Paris and was selling well, with good reviews in most major newspapers and magazines. Himes was then approached by representatives of the French television company ORTF, who wanted him to make a documentary film about life in Harlem.

Himes and the entire ORTF film crew stayed at the Theresa Hotel in Harlem. Familiar with the area, he chose the spots that he thought would be the most characteristic of everyday life in Harlem—bars, churches, beauty parlors. He also filmed a great deal about the life and politics of Malcolm X, a leading spokesman for the Black Muslims, a black nationalist group that preached separatism and racial pride. Unlike the more mainstream black leaders who were aiming toward total integration of blacks within white society, the Black Muslims believed that white society was inherently racist and that blacks must reject white society and establish their own.

Like Himes, Malcolm X had spent his youth on a crime spree that culminated in a seven-year prison term for burglary. Just as Himes had begun writing while in prison, Malcolm

X had converted to the Muslim religion and had spent his prison years studying the politics of the Nation of Islam, more commonly known as the Black Muslim movement. Upon his release from prison, he joined the Black Muslims and dropped his "slave name," Malcolm Little, to become Malcolm X.

Himes could well understand Malcolm's X's deep distrust of whites and his conviction that the white man was "the devil." However, he disagreed with Malcolm X's belief that the Muslims were the saviors of the black race. The Muslims, Himes claimed, had actually been the first to go into Africa and enslave the blacks, subsequently selling them to the Europeans.

The documentary turned out nicely, or so Himes thought. Back in Paris, he went to a screening of the edited version. He hated what the editors had done so much that he wrote a bitter article about the documentary.

Himes next went to Mexico to write a new novel, *Back to Africa*, but he returned to Paris after suffering a mild stroke. While struggling with *Mamie Mason* in 1956, he had written the synopsis for an epic novel about American blacks in Paris's Latin Quarter. The resulting book, *A Case of Rape*, was published in 1963. Essentially another autobiographical

Militant Black Muslim leader Malcolm X was a central figure in the civil rights struggle in the 1960s. Himes and a French television crew worked together on a documentary focusing in part on the life of Malcolm X.

work, *A Case of Rape* was based on Himes's relationship with Trent.

In 1963, France was still reeling from unsuccessful efforts to quell rebellion in its African colony of Algeria, which for the previous decade had been torn by terrorist fighting as the native black population fought for independence against French troops. The French government's mangled handling of the situation had cost it public confidence and political prestige. The French were very touchy on the topic of race relations at that point, and they mistook *A Case of Rape*, Himes's very personal work, for a contemporary attack on French racism. The newspaper *Paris-Presse* ran a front-page headline asking, "Are you a racist, monsieur?" and Himes became as disliked as he had briefly been appreciated.

Expatriate American artists visited Himes, as others had once come to Paris to meet the late Richard Wright. Himes's brother Joe and his wife visited on their way home from Finland, where Joe had been teaching under a Fulbright exchange program. Both brothers had nothing but praise for each other. Various groups were trying to arrange for film productions of *The Five-Cornered Square* and *A Case of Rape*, but Himes retreated to the south of France to finish *Back to Africa*, which would be published as *Cotton Comes to Harlem*.

A detective story, *Cotton Comes to Harlem* describes the efforts of Grave Digger Jones and Coffin Ed Johnson to return to the poor people of Harlem a huge sum of money they had offered to a minister who promised to lead America's black population back to their ancestral homeland. The money is hidden in a bale of cotton—hence the book's title. The idea for this story had come from the actual "Back to Africa" movement in the United States in the 1920s. Led by the Jamaican-born black nationalist leader Marcus Garvey, the movement envisioned a mass exodus of black Americans forming an independent, black-governed country in Africa. The movement had failed, and Himes felt that the very idea was preposterous. He said:

> I thought the Back to Africa program in the U.S. was one of the most absurd things the black people of America had ever supported. How were the black Americans going back to Africa? Who was to take them? Who was to support them? Protect them? Feed them? It was an opium pipe smoker's dream. But it was perfect for a con. And that was my story.

In an interview later in his life, Himes expanded on this point:

French police in Algeria search for weapons in the midst of Algeria's revolt against its French colonial rulers. The French believed that Himes's novel A Case of Rape, *published in 1963, was a comment on their treatment of the people of Algeria.*

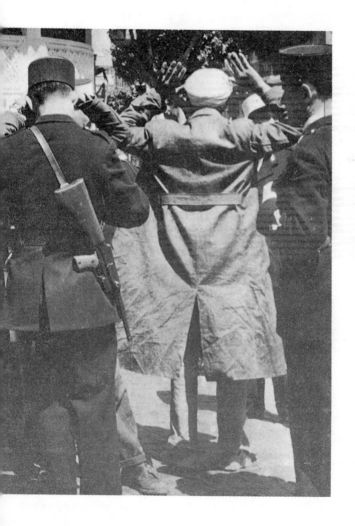

> The American black man has to make it or
> lose it in America; he has no choice. That's
> why I wrote *Cotton Comes to Harlem*. In
> Garvey's time the "Back to Africa" move-
> ment had an appeal and probably made
> some sense. But it doesn't make any sense
> now. It probably didn't make sense even
> then, but it's even *less* logical now, because
> the black people of America aren't Africans
> anymore, and the Africans don't want them.

As in his earlier detective fiction, Himes vivid-
ly depicted the harshness and brutality of life
in Harlem. He wrote to Carl Van Vechten that
this new book "goes all out on the race problem and conditions of life in Harlem, and I
have my detectives express just how they, and
the other black people, feel in Harlem."

Himes finished *Cotton Comes to Harlem* and
returned to Paris. He enjoyed his growing
celebrity, and he and Packard found themselves doing an enormous amount of entertain-
ing. Himes outlined a new book, *The God in
Me*, and proposed a short history of Harlem
for the magazine *Paris-Match*, "Anatomy of
a Ghetto," in July 1964. *Paris-Match* had re-
quested the outline, but the editors never
responded to it.

The French edition of *Cotton Comes to
Harlem* came out in 1964 and was an im-
mediate best-seller. Himes was interviewed for

the French men's fashion magazine *Adam*, and when the issue came out, there was a big color picture of him on the front cover of the magazine, which was displayed on newsstands all over the city. "After that everybody knew me by sight," he said. "I was the best-known black in Paris."

Black nationalist leader Marcus Garvey preached racial pride and sought to establish an independent black homeland in Africa in the 1920s. His views were parodied by Himes in a detective story, Cotton Comes to Harlem.

The
Aging
Expatriate

Chapter Eight

The Aging Expatriate

BY THE MID-1960s, the rights to Himes's works in America and abroad had become a tangled mess. He had never had an agent to look over both domestic and overseas rights, and his habit of constantly changing publishers did not help. In the United States, several paperback houses issued his detective novels, and it was difficult for him to obtain payment while living in Europe. In France, his relationships with the houses of Gallimard and Plon became so convoluted that they finally agreed to publish his new works in alternation. Himes finally hired an agent to oversee all his future

Himes displays the Dutch version of his novel Mamie Mason. *His books were translated into many languages, which enabled him to achieve fame throughout Europe.*

In the later years of Himes's life, he saw his work published in countless editions and literary anthologies. Black on Black *was the last of his books to be published.*

publishing arrangements.

Yet Himes now had more money than ever, and he indulged himself by purchasing a Jaguar MK 10 automobile and touring Greece with Packard, whom he finally married in late 1965. In March 1966, they moved to the south of France and rented a farmhouse in Venelles, a village outside of Aix-en-Provence. There Himes began to write what would be the first volume of his autobiography.

Samuel Goldwyn, Jr., a noted Hollywood producer, contacted Himes in 1966. He was interested in making movies out of Himes's Harlem thrillers. When Himes returned to New York in the summer of 1967 for dental work, Goldwyn flew in from California to discuss filming *Cotton Comes to Harlem*.

Goldwyn had hired a television writer to prepare the screen adaptation, but Himes was not satisfied with the resulting script. Goldwyn offered him a generous salary to write the screenplay himself. Himes believed that writing *Baby Sister* had prepared him for the assignment, so he went to work quickly, mailed the finished manuscript to Goldwyn in Hollywood, and returned to Paris.

Himes worked on his autobiography and tried to turn his relationship with Behrens into a short novel. He and Packard then moved to

Amsterdam, the Netherlands. Phil Lomax, an American writer whom Himes had met in Paris, visited the couple there and casually recounted the true story of a subway shooting in Harlem: A blind man with a gun, shooting at a man who had slapped him, missed his mark and killed an innocent bystander. Himes felt that the story was worth pursuing and put aside the novel about Behrens.

A letter arrived from Goldwyn reporting his unhappiness with Himes's script for *Cotton Comes to Harlem*. However, his enthusiasm for the project remained high. He asked Himes to come to Hollywood to work with him directly on the script, but Himes was caught up in the novel, *Blind Man with a Pistol*, that had developed out of the story Lomax told him. Unlike most crime fiction, including Himes's own, *Blind Man with a Pistol* has no conclusion. Various mysteries are pursued in alternating chapters. The characters include a 100-year-old black man, his 12 wives, their dozens of children, a fake African witch doctor, and an aging hoodlum who sets off a string of senseless murders. Coffin Ed Johnson and Grave Digger Jones want to solve these crimes, but their precinct captain is reluctant to have a scandal uncovered on the eve of his retirement. He gives them, instead, the impossible task of finding the "one man" behind a series of minor riots.

The detectives finally proclaim the culprit to be Abraham Lincoln, who freed the slaves without providing for their sustenance. This

answer does not satisfy the captain, and the detectives are sent out again to find the real culprit. When a blind man goes berserk in the subway, accidentally shooting a preacher through the heart and emerging at 125th

The United States experienced a wave of race riots in the 1960s as blacks fought for their civil rights. Himes was convinced that any gains by blacks would come only in the wake of violence.

Street waving his gun in the air, he is shot down by white policemen. A riot ensues, and Himes's detectives report that it was started by a blind man with a pistol. Told that their story does not make sense, they agree, and the novel ends.

Blind Man with a Pistol went beyond the conventional detective story genre to reflect Himes's concern with the breakdown of the social order in black America, more specifically in Harlem, and his belief that no simple solution existed to lessen the degree of chaos in the inner city or to achieve racial equality. The warring black militant groups in Himes's story wind up killing each other rather than solving the racial problem. The blind man himself, firing his pistol arbitrarily "blindly" is a metaphor for the senseless, unorganized violence sweeping the frustrated black community.

Himes finished *Blind Man with a Pistol* and mailed it to his publisher, then traveled to Spain, where he and Packard bought land and began building a house in the fishing village of Moraira. They took an apartment in nearby Alicante, and Himes began a novel called *Plan B*. Unlike *Blind Man with a Pistol*, *Plan B* would recount a real black revolution. The detectives would split up, and Grave Digger Jones would kill Coffin Ed Johnson to save the cause.

Himes continued to correspond with Goldwyn about *Cotton Comes to Harlem*. He had asked Goldwyn to find a good black playwright to do the shooting script, and Goldwyn had tried unsuccessfully to hire LeRoi Jones, a young poet and playwright whom Himes had met in New York in 1962. The problem was not Jones himself but that Goldwyn would not pay Jones the same salary he would a more seasoned writer. However, a final script, to be directed by Ossie Davis, with Raymond St. Jacques as Coffin Ed Johnson and Godfrey Cambridge as Grave Digger Jones, was hastily put together, and shooting began in April 1969.

In February 1970, Himes and Packard finally moved to their new home in Moraira. Himes was 60 years old. It was the first house he had ever owned.

Himes went to Paris in June for the opening of the film of *Cotton Comes to Harlem*, which engendered tremendous publicity. He was interviewed and profiled in the French newspaper *Le Monde*, on ORTF television, and in the American *Life* magazine, and he went to Germany to film a television profile.

Himes explained the overwhelming presence of violence in his fiction by saying, "That's one of the reasons I began writing the detective stories. I wanted to introduce the idea of violence. After all, Americans live by violence,

and violence achieves—regardless of what anyone says, regardless of the distaste of the white community—its own ends.''

In 1972, *The Quality of Hurt*—the first volume of Himes's autobiography—was

Raymond St. Jacques (left) and Godfrey Cambridge starred as Coffin Ed Johnson and Grave Digger Jones in the 1970 film version of Cotton Comes to Harlem.

published. The book covered his life in astonishing detail, from his earliest youth to the end of his affair with Trent. Only his prison life was given short shrift because he could no longer remember it clearly. He saw every phase of this part of his life as an episode of pain.

His final book of creative writings, *Black on Black: Baby Sister and Selected Writings*, was published in 1973. In addition to the screenplay of *Baby Sister* and his own choice of early short stories, the collection included two previously unpublished stories, "Tang," from 1967, and "Prediction," from 1969.

In 1974, Goldwyn produced a film of Himes's novel *The Heat's On*, calling it *Come Back, Charleston Blue*. Two years later, the second volume of Himes's autobiography, *My Life of Absurdity*, was published. His last published short story, called "Life Everlasting," was printed in a small journal in 1978.

Meanwhile, Himes had become sick with Parkinson's disease, a debilitating illness, and died on November 12, 1984, in Moraira, Spain. He was 75 years old.

All told, Himes's life was one of unusual contrasts. He was sentenced to prison as a lowly criminal, yet he rose to great heights as a noted author. He was deeply concerned with changing the condition of blacks in America, yet he lived much of his life abroad. He struggled with the publishing industry and the critical establishment throughout his literary career, yet his determination to write honestly inspired other black writers. He was a serious-minded artist, yet he did not achieve fame and respect until he wrote detective fiction. Such ironies did not escape Chester Himes, who produced a body of literature that tells the truth about the lives of blacks in America as forcefully and completely as any other protest writer.

Himes has created a body of literature that not only entertains but also provides a powerful indictment of racism in America.

CHRONOLOGY

FURTHER READING

Himes, Chester. *My Life of Absurdity.* New York: Doubleday, 1976.

_____. *The Quality of Hurt.* New York: Doubleday, 1972.

Lundquist, James. *Chester Himes.* New York: Ungar, 1976.

Milliken, Stephen F. *Chester Himes: A Critical Appraisal.* Missouri: University of Missouri Press, 1976.

Williams, John A. "My Man Himes." *Flashbacks: A Twenty-Year Diary of Article Writing.* New York: Anchor Press/Doubleday, 1973, pp. 292-352.

INDEX

PICTURE CREDITS

M. L. WILSON was born in New Orleans, Louisiana. He is a writer who specializes in nonfiction for young adults and currently lives in New York City.

NATHAN IRVIN HUGGINS is W.E.B. Du Bois Professor of History and Director of the W.E.B. Du Bois Institute for Afro-American Research at Harvard University. He previously taught at Columbia University. Professor Huggins is the author of numerous books, including *Black Odyssey: The Afro-American Ordeal in Slavery, The Harlem Renaissance,* and *Slave and Citizen: The Life of Frederick Douglass.*

MELROSE SQUARE
BLACK AMERICAN SERIES

Melrose Square proudly announces a new series of Black American biographies. Each volume is profusely illustrated, meticulously researched, widely acclaimed. The first four titles are now available. Quality paperback format: $3.95 each.

PAUL ROBESON: ATHLETE, ACTOR, SINGER, ACTIVIST. Written by Scott Ehrlich, this is the story of the gifted man who went from All-American football player at Rutgers (where he graduated first in his class) to win worldwide respect as a performer.

ELLA FITZGERALD: FIRST LADY OF AMERICAN SONG. Written by Bud Kliment, this beautifully-told biography traces Ella's fascinating life from her birth in Virginia to her White House—and international—acclaim as America's "First Lady of Song."

NAT TURNER: PROPHET AND SLAVE LEADER. Written by Terry Bisson. Fiery preacher, militant leader—and prophet—Nat Turner organized a slave uprising that struck a defiant blow against slavery in the United States thirty years before the Civil War.

JACKIE ROBINSON: FIRST BLACK IN PROFESSIONAL BASEBALL. Written by Richard Scott. The story of the man who was good enough, professional enough and, most of all, man enough to be selected to break the "color barrier" in professional baseball.

RICHARD PRYOR
THE MAN BEHIND THE LAUGHTER

BIOGRAPHY—The most famous comedian in America today—
and the most controversial—Richard Pryor's life story reads
like a work of exciting, if improbable fiction. His self-confessed
beginnings in Peoria, Illinois, where his mother was a prosti-
tute in his grandmother's bordello; his life on the streets as a
young man; his sturggle to break into show business on his

own uncompromising terms; his
acknowledged use of cocaine and
other drugs; and his near brush
with death after a mystery fire at
his home in California have all pro-
vided material for his shocking
comic portrayals. If the past is an
indicator of the future, Pryor will
continue to shock, titillate and
make the world laugh with him for
many years to come.

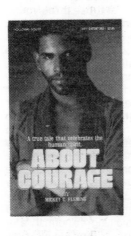

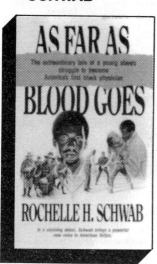

HARLEM

Harlem . . . The 1930s . . . It was the end of prohibition and Lenox Avenue was the place where sophisticates went to play. It was also the place where white gangsters and crooked cops came to collect their pounds of flesh.

When bandleader Sam Webster and his band opened their own nightclub they soon found themselves caught in the middle, with hands—and guns—coming at them from every direction. Sam and the band were great musicians, but they didn't know a helluva lot about fighting. They had to learn fast. In **Harlem** Tim McCanlies has beautifully captured the Harlem of the 1930s, that era just before black performers "moved downtown."

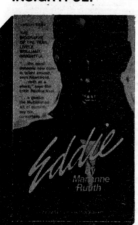